IN A ROOM
DARKENED

D0120728

Kevin Williamson

TWO RAVENS
P R E S S

Published by Two Ravens Press Ltd
Green Willow Croft
Rhiroy
Lochbroom
Ullapool
Ross-shire IV23 2SF

www.tworavenspress.com

ISBN: 978-1-906120-07-8

British Library Cataloguing in Publication Data. A CIP record for this book can be obtained from the British Library.

Designed and typeset in Sabon by Two Ravens Press.
Cover artwork by Emer Martin.

Printed on Forest Stewardship Council-accredited paper by Biddles Ltd., King's Lynn, Norfolk.

About the Author

Kevin Williamson is author of one previous book, *Drugs and the Party Line*. He was founder and editor of the Rebel Inc publishing house. *In A Room Darkened* is his first collection of poetry.

Acknowledgements

I'd like to thank the Scottish Arts Council who awarded me a Writer's Bursary in 1995 which helped find time to write/think about some of the earlier poems in this collection.

I'd like to thank the people at the National Library of Scotland who saw fit to award me the 2005 Robert Louis Stevenson Award. This bought me some precious time and space at Hotel Chevillon in Grez-sur-Loing to work on this collection.

I'd like to thank the editors of the following publications/ websites where some of these poems first appeared: Cencrastus, Chapman, HibeesBounce.com, Hybrid, LauraHird.com, New Writing Scotland, Norman MacCaig's 85th Birthday Anthology, One O'Clock Gun, Oral, Two Sevens, The Red Wheelbarrow and West Coast Magazine.

I'd like to thank Anna Battista for arranging to have one of these poems projected on to the wall of a traditional Roman Catholic chapel in Pescara, Italy, as part of an arts festival there.

And finally I'd like to thank my good friend Gael Roblin for giving me the use of his house in Plian, in the beautiful Breton countryside, to edit the collection and pull it all together. Much appreciated. One day your people will have their freedom. Breizhiz' war zav!

Kevin Williamson
Plian
Brittany
October 2006

to Anja

Contents

IN A ROOM DARKENED

REQUIEM FOR LA BELLE ANGELE

PART ONE

IN A ROOM DARKENED

A DIFFERENT KIND OF LOVE

You make me feel
like I could stand
on the domed eyelid
of our troposphere
40,000 feet up
toes curled soft
around the roof
of the blackest cumulo-
nimbus cloud ever
and dive straight in.

This is no big deal.
Nature's fury
does not scare me.
Not lightning blades
three foot thick,
not a furnace made of
tiny fishhooks,
nor jackboot thunder
that goes in one ear
and out through my arse.

I would go face-to-face
with demonic mist
scarlet-eyed jackals
& the wretched of the sky
because, well, I love you,

1

and you tell me
I would float downwards
like a butterfly
to the mossy fields below.

ADVISING A PHILISTINE

The venereal scribe,
barrel spent and satisfied,
lays down his piece
and yawns of owls and cats
and romantic comedies.
Make it new, says Ezra Pound.
Channel Bravo is the place for repeats.
I add my own tuppence worth:
      Ahem…
easy rhymes are no highway
to the complexities of the human soul.
There is a yearn beyond
metrics, comparison and wit.
      And fuck the rich.
Is that so, he sneers.
      Aye.
Anything else?
      Aye…
      if in doubt
      leave it out.
In his Beechgrove Garden dotage
he tends to his metaphors
but says nothing.
You know, it would be churlish
to hand him a cheese-grater
to scrape away the thin veneer of meaning.

AMSTERDAM LULLABY

On my back I see three black chimney pots
perched
on the roof through my third storey tenement

window   two large ones on the
outside
and a small one   in the middle

late Chet Baker blowing through the speakers
middle-finger
depressed   holds the perfect summer note

ANJA WITH A JAY

What kind of person
would fall in love
with a six foot
conger eel?

Can you imagine
trying to hold on
to a slippery Gordian
knot with teeth?

A man would need
eyes in the back
of his cock
a swivel neck

and if he could not
balance on the dart
of a pharmaceutical needle
he would be dust.

What kind of person
hunts fish anyway?
Steady hands, bait,
this is not enough.

I know all of this.
I've tickled salmon
on their pudgy guts
but only made them laugh.

I've seen deer
puzzled by nature
stop to lick semen
from a forest floor.

Last night I dreamt
I was a bear cub
prowling round the ankles
of de Milo made flesh.

Anja, through the smoke
and these mirrors.
All your little animals
are so clever and fierce.

BEFORE THE FALL

Imagine a time
of broken glass
a seven year itch
and micro proteins
wriggling around
in a primordial
chicken soup
like bad-tempered
sperm.

The most sullen
of drunken loves
will stumble home
to hatch terrible plots
against nature.

Enough is enough
is implied
even in the gentlest
of words.
Then a silence
and talk of flight.
Equilibrium
comes at a price.

Adam and Eve will argue
over anything.
The Atlantic Ocean
is green not blue
and soft as a ghost.
There is no way
you can walk across
its surface.

To America
the land of the free
migratory birds
with little choice
in the matter
oblivious
to every obstacle
in their path.

On the other
side of the world
they step past
security guards
armed with semi-
automatic weaponry
and lose each other
in the cells of Alcatraz.

The guide book says
escape is not possible.

CANUTE

From the depths
I close in on your beach
with all the patience of a shark.

What happens
next is sun and moon.
My lips foam with desire.

I crash
a ferocious kiss.
Embrace and explode.

♦ ♦ ♦

On the belly of your sand
I leave a splash of
curdled surf.

I try not to look back but
fuck, that was us.
Together.

There are always waves. They
will pound your shore
regardless.

CHRISTINE'S POEM

When you asked me
to write you a poem

I cringed
'it doesn't work like that'

I wanted to say
'it's not like ordering a Chinese'

and anyway
I don't do requests.

But when I felt the soft passion of love
on your beautiful lips

and when I think of the ways
you brought me back to life…

ah fuck it.
This one's for you.

COMPARISON

the desert rain
the river breeze
the fur of a wasp
the egg of an eye
the salt-filled seas
the mountain spring
the volcano's breath
the embers and the fire
the centre of a snowflake
the poems and the fragments
the coiled steel of a python's sleep
the blood red rose in the barrel of a gun
the motionless wings of an eagle in flight
the dead man's shark eye stare at the
faraway stars in a limitless sky

    the height
     and the
     depth
     of it all

all of these things
all of them

CONCRETE POETRY

dark clouds
over

head in the
sky

a wall to
be

finished on the
ground

all that cement
to

be moved
aye

so much depends
upon

a red wheel
barrow

CONVERSATION WITH MY ACCOUNTANT

I'm in pretty good shape
all things considered.
I'm alive
I'm Scottish
and I'm in love.
My contact with
the Dead Sea Scrolls
has been sporadic,
at worst.
I'm okay.

My accountant is wise
beyond summation
and margins of loss.
You are in a protected zone,
he says, a minority.
Beware the angry herd.
They can sniff
happiness
from a distance
the way a shark
detects blood.

Am I rich? I ask.
Have I made my fortune?
He takes off his glasses
lays them on the table
and looks me straight in the eye.
No.

EUREKA

Gram Parsons sang of brass buttons,
green silks and silver shoes.
But when I think of you

it is a pair of blue tracky bottoms
I remember most. With soldier
stripes. And a hole in the crotch.

Your hair was a mess and your armpits
smelled. But you came into my life
like a greater Christ than Dylan.

I couldn't believe my eyes.
The dance of the seven veils
does not compare with the way

you toppled over in a drunken heap
pants around your ankles.
It was a post-clubbing manoeuvre

you had down to a fine art.
Faced with the sunny delights
of your naked ass, and you, in a coma,

I did what any other red-blooded male
would do. I couldn't help myself.
I fell head over heels in love.

GEORGE BEST
(ON THE EVE OF DESTRUCTION)

Tomorrow you will die.
The whole world knows this
and there are no more excuses.

How will the scales cope?
The good the bad the foolish
and Homeric are all there

weighed in grams and shrugs.
Where did it all go wrong?
your epitaph and noose

hung beside an old pair of
ruby slippers. But your gift
lingers on, like perfume

conjured from the dreamiest
Belfast air. In terminal decline
you scored three times for the Hibs.

1980. I saw one. You cut in
from the West Stand, stepped to
the right, perfect balance, body

weight on your left foot, flashed
a thunderous shot into the Celtic goal.
Some things last forever. Thank you.

GIVE THE BOY A COCONUT

John Ashbery, poet, you have no master.
Silver plaudits rain down in waterfalls

plop, plop, a deluge of showered praise
as wet as any shuddering nymph's fanny.

*'Truly the shooting star of contemporary
verse,'* pronounce your learned friends.

'Suck on this bitch' such mysterious words.
You don magician's cloak and deposit them

in tangents, vagueness, and wanton erudition.
By Jupiter, the man can even speak Latin!

John Ashbery, your inner lyric peacock things
are fine monuments to themselves. Amazing.

Like Rod Stewart, you wear your genius well.
You truly are The Emperor of Verse.

HYMN TO KARL MARXISM

In the playful years
before polemics and beards
could tickle a girl's fancy
the boy genius could not bear
the pedantic quibbles
of a fussing mother
nor the iron rod
of patriarchal power.
'Come on, Karl, eat your vegetables.'

Karl would tease his sisters
and pull their hair –
they had such lovely hair.

Sometimes silenced
he would sulk and rage
and bluster and growl
before burying
his wounded pride
in the dust of economics
and the battle weary dialectic
of love and hate.

Yet when Darwin cried 'ape'
and the earth was made scarlet
it was a child's impotence
that drove such a furious pen.

'The state will wither away'
was a music hall joke of the time
much loved by the plotters
of Cartesian resistance.

*'The proletariat have nothing to lose
but their chains'*
got less laughs
but more votes.

In its fevered jaws
dripping with the blood of want
and the victor's conceit
History will tell us that
the beer was much stronger
in the salons of imperial Prussia
and the ladies demure
behind their twitching fans.

*'Let the ruling class tremble
at revolution'*
went the rallying call.
That may be so.
But who would trust a prophet
who wished his mother dead
(for the money)
and who couldn't find time
to bury his father's corpse.

IN A ROOM DARKENED

In a room darkened

> I'm out there among the satellite debris — the DNA
> twists of genetic lucky charms — the molecular
> depths and the infra-yellow heights — the blue-
> white centres of the blackest black holes — the
> rotated crosses on empty graves — the parried
> swords and the hacking switchblades — & the
> razor nails on the steel fingers of the slashing
> hands that push, cut, shred, through the guilt of
> space that tears between the you that is me and
> the me that is you

In a room darkened

> I cling to the honey — the black treacle — the
> back-throat sherbet — the scented fur — the lycra
> tingle — the hot metallic blood — the aniseed lick
> — & the last gasp bumper to bumper kiss of all
> the flat earth of your skin that covers me morning,
> noon and night

In a room darkened

> I forget the death watch beetles lying on their
> backs, legs waving, feeler eyes grinning — the
> turquoise damp on the crumbling walls of a

transplant heart — the icy blasts of vanishing
trains — the ammonia cut of low-grade crack —
the shrivelled breasts on a tiger's tongue
strike — the last venal entrance to Eva Braun's
corpse — the body bags of restricted joy — &
the dusty winged moths that flutter across my
eyes as they open their slits to the torn
chrysalis of your still-born love that is me

In a room darkened

I love you with the ivory bite of mouth
on mouth — the parallel spear of four blue
eyes — the electric burn of eight limbs
fused — the fingertip brush — the arc on
arc — the liquid flames — & the sad long
rush of a revolution's breath as your siren
queen divests her robes for the naked
warmth of my republic's embrace

JUST LIKE YOU

The way ducks
will follow ducks

the way sheep
will follow sheep

I come back to MacCaig
the way MacCaig

returns to his many frogs
and his Highland streams.

The man is no more dead (to me)
than Wallace or Burns

or my friend Sandie
who sleeps in a call box

her pretty arms full of poetry
and passion and blood.

However, I reserve the right
to argue with anyone

even in their absence.
It is the Celtic way.

In one ill-considered jibe
you refer to Robert The Bruce

as a 'Norman.' No way!
He was as Scottish as you or me.

And besides
be careful with your insults.

MOVING STATUE
(BEN BHRAGGIE AT DUSK)

It could be anything
the light on the hill.

The brightest firefly in the universe!

This hill with its gentle
slopes and its back

to the barren wasteland
of vanished people.

Its sheep are like dandruff.

On a pedestal stands the duke
at the summit of his powers

casting his stony eye
to the north sea, to his castle.

Dunrobin? Fuckin right he is.

Aye, it could be anything
the light on the hill.

A match struck? Dynamite?
Here's hoping.

24

MURDER IN GLASGOW

There was never the poem
that needed introduction.

Like this one. Set in concrete
shoes on the floor of the River Clyde.

Its mouth is closed. Like the yards.
Like the private gardens.

Time after time there are bubbles
of thought to the surface.

Continue, they glug, continue to flood
this town with all that it seeks.

Taggart, you won't find anyone
in this poem who has a clue.

MY FAVOURITE RAIN

is the one where sunlight
sparkles in every droplet

where the sky is the blue-grey
reflection of your blue-grey eyes

where the thunder purrs
the syllables of your name.

my favourite rain falls
indoors, in your bedroom,

inside the parched matrix
of your beautiful mind.

my favourite rain never
touches the ground

it hangs, on your words,
forever.

MY MIND IS LIKE MY BED

always in a mess
never made up
but empty
without you

NIGHT TIME BENEATH THE BRIDGE

how does he do that
all night long?
lips pursed raw
the brass instrument dissolving
in his grubby white fingers
blowing troubled mellow
like some street punk jigaboo.

the straight life
is skewed into
grudged applause
Art takes a bow
up there on his pedestal
night time beneath the bridge.

high above and out of sight
the west end girls
ruffle their hair
corn ears turned inside-out
whispering behind porcelain fingers:
    'ooh la la, bay-bee!'

but Art plays on
mirror shades and scars:
    'oh that morning sun'
awake regardless
of the rundown red

of a new dawn chorus
fresh rolls and a cardboard rustle
notes plucked from thin air
echoing through empty streets
how does he do it?

Art never tires
just connects
sulph blues at arms length
lids sealed tight
sees nothing
fingers dance a pirouette
hypnotising a girl
on a far out trip:
'you know, I never seeeeeen
such a sad sound'
she sighs
leaping kinda crazy
round a bucket fire
beside the war memorial.

NORMAN MACCAIG (AT 85)

Tortoise is great.
I love the way it comes into its own
as post-party animal
of the chill-out terrain;
as time-served stress-buster
even more so than
the dull-witted goldfish
with its seven-second brain
and mouth permanently a-gawp.

Tortoise does not care to indulge
in movement-based analogies.
Just a quiet nod of its dinosaur head
the slow plod of leaden foot
and sleep – all or nothing repose –
like Auld Reekie
shutting up shop for winter.

Tortoise is beauty
the steady accumulation of poetry
grown older and wiser,
savouring the textures of its native soil.

Tortoise does not live forever
(though it may seem so)
but gradually retreats into its shell
with the passing years
absorbed in its own
internal dynamics.

Tortoise has no need
to puff its chest,
nor leap and roar.
Remember the hare!

ONE DOWN

Your voice was soft and hesitant,
the door a perfect frame for
the lemon twist of your words:

'Could you at least put down the
paper and listen to what I'm saying.
The crossword can wait.'

Conjugal Join? Mental cogs whirred
as I sifted through the swamp of
consonants and vowels. *Conjugal Join?*

'I've had enough. I'm leaving. If space is
what you want, then space is what you've
got. But you'll have to fill it without me.'

The words echoed empty in the hall. I heard
a taxi door slam in the distance. Of course!
Colloquial slang. Four letters. As in off.

OPEN-TOE SANDALS ARE COOL

When I asked my girlfriend
to wash my feet
with her hair
she told me to fuck off
and who did I think I was
some kinda sexist pig?

I laid a biblical rap on her
come on, I said,
it's erotic as fuck
I read it in the bible
Mary Magdalene
she done it for Jesus
so why can't you do it for me...

She eyed me suspicious
and asked if that was the whore
Jesus shacked up with
pre-crucifixion
and worse
thought I was calling *her* a whore
naw, naw, it's religious, I explained
a ceremony, an act of love.

She said that
in her version of the bible
(The King James)
the lead character of Christ
did not wear three day old socks
and dirty trainers.
I suppose she had a point.

ORDER OF IMPORTANCE

'Your LPs are in no particular order.'
You are so fucking wrong, mate.

'How can you find one when there are so many?'
Wrong again. On both counts.

'Would it not be better to arrange them ...'
Go on, say it.

'... in alphabetical order?'
They're in the order I like them.

'It wouldn't take long.'
That's because it won't happen, pal.

'I don't understand you.'
Good. Let's keep it that way.

PAGES TORN FROM A HISTORY DENIED

1707

The Edinburgh mob was a fearsome sight
When they chased the traitors in the night
The great and good who would not fight
    For Scotia's liberty.
They grabbed their gold then took to flight
    To damned Eternity.

1746

A song from Seventeen Forty-Four
The year before the Highland roar
An anthem for the English score
    God Save Their German King.
A dirge to praise an ugly sore
    Which only slaves will sing.

1793

Thomas Muir his head unbowed
Dunbar the Brit he bellowed loud
The hangman wishing for a crowd
    To while the hours away.
But Muir escaped no spirit kowed
    To fight another day.

1803

Cannons makes an awful stench
Acrid fumes and limbs a-wrench
The Iron Duke behind the trench
    His slaughter never ends.
But hell with war we love the French
    Their Revolution's friends.

1820

Who sings of Hardie, Wilson, Baird
And how the Eighteen-Twenty fared
And who was rattled who was scared
    As weavers wove their truth.
The British axe and teeth were bared
    To shut the poorest mooth.

1822

The tartan tat Sir Walter gave
To dress us like a happy slave
And with it manners to behave
    Like an Englishman abroad.
But till I'm covered by the grave
    I will not buy this fraud.

1919

A war was won but lives were lost
The landlords couldn't give a toss
They joined hands with every boss
    To hang us out to dry.
Then tanks rolled in past Glasgow Cross
    To smother freedom's cry.

POETRY HAS GONE SOFT

Poetry has gone soft.
Soft as Peter Sutcliffe's cock
in its inability to shock.

Poetry has gone weak.
Its head buried, like an ostrich,
so far up its own ass
it has two beaks.

Poetry has drowned.
Drowned in a sea of pricks
where even the rhymes stick
in the craw
as harmless metrical flaws.

O where is the poetry
that splashes its delight
on your face
like a hooker's piss?

RAPUNZEL

The solitude and years have
built a wall around your heart.

Breeze blocks were piled high
to create a perfect turret.

In the dark you stare out into space
tugging at Orion's belt.

One day you'll be gone.
Bluebirds will fill the air.

Beneath your window
I'll keep jumping and cursing

to the point of foolishness
somehow expecting the sight

of your shaved head
to appear at the battlements.

SADISM FOR BEGINNERS

What would melt the ice in your eyes
and the winter in your veins?
It is an important question.
As vital as garlic and oxygen
or the polaroids that make me blush.

Yesterday, gold was satin sheets,
warm towels, and a jacuzzi,
beside a box of plastic sex toys.

Now, if I suggest Sunday morning skin,
a pink Rolls Royce,
or diamonds the size of cataracts
placed on the blank of your stare
this would be a slur, a desecration.

Then there is the question of knives
to be considered. Twisted in ventricles.
I realise, too late, that the pain of fear
is much greater than the fear of pain.

Your choice is to agonise, like Justine,
in her French dungeon, as I hang
with a noose around my throat,
awaiting the grace of your hesitant blade.

SECOND HYMN TO KARL MARXISM

Set the end of the world on the one hand
against a man with toothache on the other.

So it must have seemed to the crippled Moor
drenched in the sting of an iodine apocalypse.

In a room nearby, an integral component
of a man's materialist soul cries out:

'Karl, my strength is ebbing.'

Alas, the pedestrian par excellence
could not rouse his broken frame.

There would be no goodbye, no rhetorical
flourish, no last revolt against the status quo.

The aged Moor would sail to Gaza
have his head shaved, and his beard removed.

Highgate Cemetery. A year later.
Eleven old men remove their caps.

It's easy to shake one's fist in the air
and make a wish.

The ruling class don't do much trembling

these days. More's the pity for that.

Perhaps, one day, the complacent sentinels
of their own utopia will also cry out:

'Karl, my strength is ebbing.'

SOMEBODY'S DONE FOR
(Ted Hughes & Sylvia Plath Cut Up/Joined Together)

His ankles, bound with sacking and hairy band,
roped in at the end by the one

crossing into power,
terrify me, they seem so old.

But the warm weight of his breathing
shadows our safety –

a rat that goes on screeching,
a living doll, everywhere you look.

Across clearings, an eye,
that knocks me out:

an apparition in camouflage, an assertion in doubt –
it is like possessing a saint.

He shivers for feel of the world licking his side.
I am guilty of nothing.

SOMETHING GOT LOST SOMEWHERE
ALONG THE WAY

Yesterday I sat on the bank
of an artificial lake
and watched a toad
half submerged, half asleep.
Three hours later and
the toad had barely moved.

This toad has too much time
on its hands, I thought.
Its heartbeat bubbled.
An occasional blink
of two dome eyes.
A reposition of its legs.

Visitors were curious.
Three geese paddled past,
greedy perhaps, inquisitive,
found nothing and left –
a trail of minor vees
broke the surface tension.
The toad blinked.

This corner of France
has dragonflies the size
of hummingbirds.
These peacocks of the air
do helicopter swivels
and shimmer blue
the colour of dreams.

I love the way
tiny quicksilver fish
nibble on algae
like old ladies.
The water is clear enough
to see the fish
know exactly
what they are doing.

Three hours pass.
Or maybe it was five.
The toad had me beat.
One of us felt the death
of a yellow sun
dragging its sorry ass
across a pale blue sky.

What is there to change?
Aujourd'hui, je suis très occupé.
Yesterday, there was nothing to do.

STUART CHRISTIE

The sixth Beatle emerged
from the fires of a Spanish hell
and smiled!

All hail, the boy
with the bomb in his eyes.

Sixty-seven was a time
for fireworks.

Jim Baxter and Malcolm X.
Sonny Barger
and Jock Stein.

Actions speak louder than words.

*'I aint got no quarrel
with the Viet Cong.'*

Prison is a state of mind.
I hope you sent a postcard.

To The Generalissimo
From Scotland
With Love
xxx

THE FOOL ON CALTON HILL

He was sitting down
wearing his Spaceship Earth T-shirt
and he asks me:
How do you think we should free Scotland?

I says:
General strikes,
millions on the streets,
and distribute Kalashnikovs.

And still sitting down
he says:
Yeah, I'd vote for that.

THE LAST PICTURE SHOW

The skies are on fire

The trees have sunk roots
   of tangled blue
   & there's thunder in your head.

Vincent Van Gogh
   have the crows come
   to peck out your eyes?

THE LOVERS

'Hello' he said.

'Hello' she said.

'I'd like to go to bed with you' he said.

'I'd like to go to bed with you, too' she said.

'I love you' he said.

'I love you, too' she said.

'I'd like to marry you' he said.

'I'd like to marry you, too' she said.

'I've drawn you a picture' he said.

'I've drawn you a picture, too' she said.

'I like your picture' he said.

'I like your picture, too' she said.

'I'd like to read a book now' he said.

'I'd like to read a book now, too' she said.

'I don't think it's a very good book' he said.

'I don't think it's a very good book, too' she said.

'I'd like a cup of tea' he said.

'I'd like a cup of tea, too' she said.

'I don't take milk' he said.

'I don't take milk, too' she said.

'I'd like a peperami stick shoved up my arse' he said.

'I'd like a peperami stick shoved up my arse, too' she said.

'I enjoyed that' he said.

'I enjoyed that, too' she said.

'I think I'll jump off a four hundred foot cliff' he said.

'I think I'll jump off a four hundred foot cliff, too' she said.

'I'm going to do it right now' he said.

'I'm going to do it right now, too' she said.

'I'll always love you' he said.

'I'll always love you, too' she said.

He took a long, last look at her, kissed her on the cheek, and whispered in her ear: 'Right then ... you first.'

THE LUMINOUS FLAME OF ROSIE SAVIN

When she talks of her art
and that orange light glows
inside her palemoon head
I'm like a worm on a hook.

Her favourite colours   (she tries to explain)
are like Chinese whispers.
Imagine John Coltrane (she says)
through the damp of an Edinburgh haar.

Her brushstrokes   (she fills her lungs with smoke)
are a pastel jazz and charcoal grey.
She says primitive at best   (exhale)
but it's trance that does the trick.

I study her *Landscape of Lips*
and see Saturn's rings,
Lon Chaney's eyes, pinks
and a private antechamber to hell.

I don't really understand
why the hairs on my neck
stiffen as she sings
that faraway song of herself.

THE MAN WHO WOULD BE KING

Walt Disney
had a use for mirrors,
vanity, cocaine,
and for his queen;
a wicked glimpse
of the future.

The cartoon logic
of America
found its pale reflection,
reversed,
in the sun tan
permafrost of a Pinocchio
who couldn't keep
his cock in his trousers.

The stoic French
had a name for
Louis XI:
'The Universal Spider.'
Loathed by all
he wove a royal web
of rape, corruption,
lies and deceit.

Walt Disney
called his own Louis
'King of the Swingers'
greedy with desire
for man's red fire.
But his hairy arms
and power-crazed eyes
were no match
for a honey drunk bear.

Legends say
that to break a mirror
brings seven years
bad luck. Sure.
This is tough.
But to look
in the same glass
and see what is truly there?
How hard is that?

TO BE PERFECTLY FRANK

Joy without sadness
is inconceivable.

Just as pleasure without pain
can only be a shadow
of its own possibilities.

Likewise, I need Scotland
framed
by the neighbours from hell

and my heart torn out
by your own fair hands.

This is why I stand
at Easter Road
on a winter's night

with poetry and love
in my soul

the moon and the stars
in a velvet sky

a world of infinite before me
a world of spectacle around me

and scream

with all that is beautiful
and perfect about the human race:

'Get into those Jambo bastards...'

TREE OF KNOWLEDGE

I want to know you
I want to really know you

the way
a twisted vine
will grow
to know
its only wall

the way
a snowflake
will melt
just once
in the air
as it falls

the way
an electron
is fixed
to its sub-
atomic pair

the way
the night
knows
the sun
will always
be there

I want to know you
I want to really know you

TRICKY ONE

Just the other day
I was pondering
on the mysteries of life
as you do

wondering
what came first
Tom Leonard
or Irn Bru?

UNIVERSAL TRUTHS

The earth is round.
The sky is blue.
Snails crawl.

To state the obvious
is an art form perfected
by idiots.

Scotland is too poor.
Scotland is too small.
Scotland is too afraid.

These are a set
of universal truths
cast in stone.

Yet the world is no sphere.
It is flat at both poles.
How can this be?

And the infinite sky
is but a dark reflection
of daylight and sea.

We Scots carry our country
on our back.
We will not crawl
to independence.

VANISHING POINT

Even in dreams you pull away
your flickering eyes betray you.
It didn't seem much to begin with
just another cross on a pauper's grave.

As we travelled through miles of desolate
Caithness marsh you were gone.
I stared at the flat roads and felt
the prickle of holly and forget-me-nots.

I watched you light a cigarette
and turn flames into a soft grey ash.
I could feel it in my veins, the way
the curlews swooped and screeched.

On the gentle slopes of Bettyhill
you picked sharpened whins
and drove them into my skin.
There were no soft drugs involved.

We came to a halt at Tongue. Alone
on the shore, I went down on my knees
to pray for cockles and mussels and pearls.
You filed your nails with a board.

Something terminal and sad was written
in the way you walked along the beach,
as if backwards, through hands of bracken.
You wore a crown of tangled gorse.

The tide was gone, leaving miles
of corrugated sand. So we waited.
Five days I counted. Then five years.
There was something I forgot to say.

WHAT A HOWLER

I've seen the best minds of a generation
quietly destroyed by old age
their electro-neural processes
finally focused on the empty page

Ginsberg's *Om* going on and on
into some sort of Bodhivistian grace
and Timothy Leary's *Why Not?*
floating off into outer space

which only left Burroughs:
an octogenarian stew at 82
and still sharp as a tack

and all I can think is:
you should have stuck with the drugs
Jack Kerouac.

WISHING FOR A NEW LIFE
(Scene from the Braes Hotel, Stromness)

the sun
set alight at dusk

the life
slow as a junkie's walk

the boat
drifting out the harbour

(the wide blue V
on a still blue sea)

the talk
rhythmic in the bar

thoughts
as clear as the waters

and you
dreamy-eyed and tranquil

breathing in
         breathing out

breathing in
         breathing out

XMAS EVE LAMENT

There is a fake pine tree
in every bar in town

shedding needles
on plastic breasts.

Unopened mail weighs
heavy on my conscience

and the lipstick smear
want no one but themselves.

Hark! The amateur drunks
whisper mistletoe clichés

in glitterball ears. The marzipan
slush fills with butterball sick.

You wanna know something?
Wizard and Slade

are really getting on ma tits.
It's A Wonderful Life?

Yeah, sure.
But the fat angels are high

on tequila, and the reindeers
full of Eskimo piss.

I can hear church bells ringing.
And choir boys singing.

Holy Mother of Jesus.
Pass me the Asti Spumante.

ZEBRAS

Hey you!
Don't cry.

There are many
different ways
to say goodbye.

Horses for courses?
Perhaps.

Like you I like horses.
Especially zebras.

They make me smile
and everything
is black and white
for a while.

Sit back.
Relax.
Life is a canter.

See ya around.
Kxxx

PART TWO

REQUIEM FOR LA BELLE ANGELE

REQUIEM FOR LA BELLE ANGELE

1.

The rubble and colours and sunlight
and the burned out beating heart
are all that's left now.
The Cowgate treats her dead
with typical disdain.
Connolly, the hero
of all Ireland, is invisible
but for a plaque on a wall
that could say anything
from a distance.
The trail of blood that led
to the waspish sting
in the flesh of Ahmed Shek
has long since dried
into an eternal stain
on Edinburgh's restless soul.
This corner of Auld Reekie is like
the *Bad Lieutenant* meets
The Invasion of the Body Snatchers.

2.

In this schizophrenic city of ours
among the damp vaults
and broken bottles
beneath the neoclassical shadows

of Robert Adam
and the tramp of Cromwell's boots
we stagger into the pleasurezone
of Manga's breakbeat science.
That first gracious night with you
Jesus Christ it was religious
the smell and taste of your sweat
got me so fuckin horny
it was like climbing on board
the Titanic, waiting
for the inevitable flood
of gin and ice,
and not a lifeboat in sight.

3.

It was never going to last.
We both knew it from the start.
But hey the bass pulverised our hearts
the way a fat-faced chef kneads dough
and I could feel apples
crashing on our heads
'it's called gravity, mate'
and it only needed
the lightest of touch
the softest of breath
the most careless of lips
yet no matter how hard I danced
the angelic state of being
that shamanistic holiest of joys
was as elusive

as a white ghost
in a white machine
although it has to be said
– in our defence –
we came so damn close
to touching the stars.

4.

I remember the night
the original Grandmaster Flash
on the wheels of steel
came all the way
from New York City,
hung his mike into the crowd,
dark shades and beret,
and had the whole joint singing
'Europe... Endless...'

5.

A lot of laughter died in that fire.
We should've seen the smoke signals
that terrible night
sat among the shadows, dust
and embarrassed coughs
in a diaspora of gloom
it was agony,
pure agony, watching
Phil Kay
the funniest guy in town

losing it on stage:
'I'm gonna shut my eyes
and count to ten,
and when I open them
I want youse all to be gone.'
We couldn't move. Nobody did.
We stayed to watch a cruel dagger
sink into the heart
of the last romantic clown.
The signs were there, only
we didn't know how to read them.

6.

When the film was over
I admired the way
Jean Cocteau
made his Beast
mourn and whimper:
'Adieu, La Belle.'

7.

Like sex or death
or Shakespearean love
the exit
was never going to be
easy.
But the entrance –
now that was a sight!
Zigzagging

past the cloak room
through a crowded tunnel
suspended in time
a corridor of light and dark
a muffled sound
a table to the left
toilets to the right
down the steps
slow
      baby
           slow

almost there...
                then we're in!

Hey...

All the DJs...
All the Superstars...

Paul! Innes! Irvine! Pete!
Ange! Krissy! Rosie! Tam!
Russell! Henry! Mikey! Jim!
Gary! Gaye! Anji! Sam!
Charlotte! Adam! Simon! Jo!
Fiona! Trish! Rodney! Anne!
Eddie! Neil! Gordon! Roz!
Kenny! Mark! Tori! Stan!

8.

For one night only:
La Belle Angele.
The Rezerection.

Dancing in the flames
your hand in mine
we squeeze the dead ecstasy
from every last song of love

'Can you feel it?'
        'Can you feel it?'
                'Can you feeel it...?'

Yeah, I can still feel it.

SNOWBALLS IN SUMMER

I never saw leith walk
    like this before
crouched low in a silver mini
sliding down a runway
through a tunnel of dancing shifting
    yellowbulblights
the road ahead swishing
    gently to the left
    and to the right
now stretching back
    behind us
where time is lost
and all sense of direction
    is no direction...

yeah, I never saw leith walk
    like this before
the yellow street lights
    separating
    like magic
in the full light
in the fullness
in the morning
the silver car
stopped outside

BORLANDS
TELEVISION AND DARTS SHOP
(*Established 1925*)
and in the window
of this
TOTAL LEISURE EXPERIENCE
RETAIL CENTRE
reflected
    is a friend
    who's hugging me
    like I'm his brother
DARTS AND TV
    we're laughing like crazy
    like we're the only ones
    who get the joke
then it's back down the walk
    two snowmen
    rushing on air
pupils grown large as
    big black saucepan lids
    with luuuv
scooping up the snowballs
    in the summer of '93
    (and eating them)
and touching the velvet skin
    of the most beautiful
    girl in the world
thinking
    this is the way
    the world bends

CHILL BREEZE

There is a world of bedrooms in the morning.
Heads nodding to glow-stick tribal beats

hands, soft, fallen limp on plasticine chairs.
There is a sexual ache and a slow grind.

Satincladgirls and clublandfiends return from
a black furnace. You'll hear echoes of the sea

through the silver smoke, sickly yellow waterfalls,
flesh torn apart, and a north wind blown from

a purple conch. Sound is harmonised to the rock
and splash of cranial flow. And us! Each passing

kiss is little more than a drugged mouth on chapped
lips. But the comedown is visual, gentle and joy.

Poetry from Two Ravens Press

Castings
Mandy Haggith

A new collection of poems by Mandy Haggith, whose writing reflects her love for the land and her concern for the environment - not just in the North-West Highlands where she now lives on a woodland croft, but also in her travels around the world.

'The poetry here shows real clarity of eye marking the dialogues of nature in a place, be that place the lonely Scottish crofting area that is home, or the course of the River Kelvin through the Lowlands, or a Russian forest.' **Tom Leonard**

'Outstanding originality and quality. Impressive for its sharpness, sympathy and decisiveness...' **Alan Riach**

£8.99. ISBN 978-1-906120-01-6. Published April 2007.

Leaving the Nest
Dorothy Baird

A collection of poetry by Dorothy Baird that represents a woman's journey into adulthood, through childbirth and motherhood and then on, as her children grow up and she passes into menopause and beyond.

'Images, ideas and sounds fill eyes, ears, mouth and mind – and not just occasionally, but constantly. These pieces are the outpouring of a remarkable talent. They inhabit this universe in all its aspects: seasons, elements, animals, birds, land and sea. They are unobtrusively urgent, unashamed, and alive with longing lingering thoughts and feelings, with intensely personal experiences which Dorothy Baird has triumphantly universalised. They are an eloquent meditation on our lives, filled with the rich loam of humanity. In an increasingly ugly and unpredictable world, these poems are a reminder and an example of just how beautiful life can be.'
Christopher Rush

£8.99. ISBN 978-1-906120-06-1. Published July 2007.

The Zig Zag Woman
Maggie Sawkins

A first collection of poetry by Maggie Sawkins.

'Maggie Sawkins draws brilliantly on extended metaphor and the surreal to explore painful relationships, mental illness and problematic situations. She writes both from personal experience and beyond it. Her inventive and highly individual voice is always authentic. The taut writing carries emotional weight and sends that shiver up my spine which tells me I am reading real poetry. This is a very exciting first collection.' **Myra Schneider**

£8.99. ISBN 978-1-906120-08-5. Published September 2007.

Fiction from Two Ravens Press

Nightingale
Peter Dorward

On the second of August 1980, at 1pm, a bomb placed under a chair in the second class waiting room of the international railway station in Bologna exploded, resulting in the deaths of eighty-five people. Despite indictments and arrests, no convictions were ever secured ...

'Nightingale is a gripping and intelligent novel; it takes an unsentimental and vivid look at the lives of a small group of Italian terrorists and the naive Scottish musician who finds himself in their midst in Bologna in 1980. Full of authentic detail and texture, Nightingale *is written with clarity and precision. Peter Dorward tells this tragic story with huge confidence and verve.'* **Kate Pullinger**

£9.99. ISBN 978-1-906120-09-2. Published September 2007.

Love Letters from my Death-bed
Cynthia Rogerson

There's something very strange going on in Fairfax, California. Joe Johnson is on the hunt for dying people; the Snelling kids fester in a hippie backwater and pretend that they haven't just killed their grandfather; and Morag, multi-bigamist from the Scottish Highlands is diagnosed with terminal cancer by Manuel – who may or may not be a doctor. Cynthia Rogerson's second novel is a funny and life-affirming tale about the courage to love in the face of death.

'Witty, wise and on occasions laugh-aloud funny. A tonic for all those concerned with living more fully while we can.' **Andrew Greig**

£8.99. ISBN 978-1-906120-00-9. Published April 2007.

Parties
Tom Lappin

Gordon yearns for a little power; Richard wishes reality could match the romantic ideal of a perfect pop song; Grainne wants life to be a little more like Tolstoy. Beatrice looks on and tries to chronicle the disappointment of a generation measuring the years to the end of the century in parties.

Parties, the début novel by journalist Tom Lappin, is a scathing, insightful and profoundly human commentary on party politics and the corrupting effects of power. But above all it is a satire: a black comedy about young people getting older, and learning to be careful what they wish for, lest they end up finding it.

£9.99. ISBN 978-1-906120-11-5. Published October 2007.

Prince Rupert's Teardrop
Lisa Glass

Mary undresses and wades into the boating lake. She dives and opens her eyes. In the blur, she perceives the outline of a head – she reaches...

A dead bird. But she will keep searching. Because Mary's mother, Meghranoush – a ninety-four year-old survivor of the genocide of Armenians by the Turkish army early in the twentieth century – has vanished.

Mary is already known to the police: a serial telephoner, a reporter of wrongdoing, a nuisance. Her doctor talks of mental illness. But what has happened is not just inside her head. A trail of glass birds mocks her. A silver thimble shines at the riverbed – a thimble that belonged to her mother. A glassblower burns a body in a furnace and uses the ash to colour a vase. Rumours circulate of a monster stalking the women of Plymouth. A serial killer who specialises in the elderly.

Has Mary's mother simply left – trying to escape the ghosts of genocide in her mind – or has she been abducted? It is left to this most unreliable and unpredictable of daughters to try to find her, in this moving, lyrical, and very powerful work.

'Lisa Glass writes with dazzling linguistic exuberance and a fearless imagination.' R.N. Morris

'A virtuoso stylist of the calibre of Rachel Cusk, Lisa Glass has created a powerful murder mystery, whose violent undercurrents flow from the bitter inheritance of the Armenian genocide.'
Stevie Davies

£9.99. ISBN 978-1-906120-15-3. Published November 2007.

Short Fiction from Two Ravens Press

Highland Views: a collection of stories by David Ross

'I'm a big fan. A fine organic collection that advances a viewpoint, culture and history quite other than the urban central belt that still lopsidedly dominates recent Scottish literature.' **Andrew Greig**
£7.99. ISBN 978-1-906120-05-4. Published April 2007.

Riptide: New Writing from the Highlands and Islands Sharon Blackie & David Knowles (Eds)

This diverse collection of new fiction and poetry from the Highlands & Islands showcases the work of established writers and new names to watch.
'...a force of creation, the kind of irresistible tide into which we should dip.' **The Scotsman**
£8.99. ISBN 978-1-906120-02-3. Published April 2007.

Types of Everlasting Rest: a collection of short stories by Scotsman-Orange Prize winner Clio Gray

'Clio Gray is a master of atmosphere and sensuousness. She combines historical realism with the bizarre, whimsy with the macabre. Reading her is like being at a sumptuous feast in a palace, just before it is stormed.' **Alan Bissett**
£8.99. ISBN 978-1-906120-04-7. Published July 2007.

For more information on these and other titles, and for extracts and author interviews, see our website.

Titles are available direct from the publisher at
www.tworavenspress.com
or from any good bookshop.